MW00874893

Ask DeAvila Sadé

Presents

The Therapeutic Journal

DeAvila Sadé Bennett, LMSW

The Therapeutic Journal

I dedicate this book to all the individuals who may have thought life's obstacles had destroyed them. You were bent, but never broken.

The Therapeutic Journal

A Healing Letter to You

Greetings Doer,

I hope this letter finds you well. I called you "Doer" because when you decided to purchase this journal, you became a person that takes action. You do things. Things that are uncomfortable and downright difficult at times.
If you are completing this journal, it is because you are on a journey of self-discovery. You are attempting to make sense of some past hurts, understand some present concerns, and begin developing a road map to your future. For that alone, I applaud you. You are more courageous than you know.

I hope this journal brings about self-exploration, vulnerability, transparency, and anything else that will allow you to live your best life. I pray for your healing throughout this journey.

XOXO,
DeAvila Sadé

'How to Use the Therapeutic Journal'

To best utilize this journal, I would strongly recommend that you use it when you are relaxing in a space that is uncluttered and free of distractions. The questions require great thought and should be addressed when you are in the best mindset.

This is what I would call the "art of processing." The journal will help you process your thoughts and the emotions associated with those thoughts. This is the time where you can be the most transparent, honest, and vulnerable with yourself.

There are 30 prompts found in this journal. The journal is broken into three sections: Past, Present, and Future. Each journal entry completed should be followed by meditation, so that you can truly understand and observe how you truly feel about your self-discovery.

The Therapeutic Journal

The Therapeutic Journal

PAST

DeAvila Bennett

The Therapeutic Journal

PROMPT #1

Who has hurt you in the past and has never apologized for it?

DeAvila Bennett

The Therapeutic Journal

DeAvila Bennett

The Therapeutic Journal

DeAvila Bennett

The Therapeutic Journal

The Therapeutic Journal

PROMPT #2

Words hurt. Sometimes they leave deeper scars than actual physical wounds. Who may have hurt you with their words?

DeAvila Bennett

The Therapeutic Journal

_____

_____

_____

_____

_____

_____

_____

_____

_____

_____

_____

_____

_____

_____

_____

_____

DeAvila Bennett

The Therapeutic Journal

DeAvila Bennett

The Therapeutic Journal

_____

_____

_____

_____

_____

_____

_____

_____

_____

_____

_____

_____

_____

_____

_____

_____

DeAvila Bennett

PROMPT #3

Abandonment could be someone leaving you (a father walking out, a significant other leaving you for another person, death of a loved one, etc.)

Have you ever struggled with abandonment? How have you dealt with it?

DeAvila Bennett

The Therapeutic Journal

_____

_____

_____

_____

_____

_____

_____

_____

_____

_____

_____

_____

_____

_____

_____

_____

DeAvila Bennett

The Therapeutic Journal

DeAvila Bennett

The Therapeutic Journal

_____

_____

_____

_____

_____

_____

_____

_____

_____

_____

_____

_____

_____

_____

_____

_____

_____

DeAvila Bennett

PROMPT #4

What advice would you tell your teenage self?

Do you follow that advice today?

DeAvila Bennett

The Therapeutic Journal

_____

_____

_____

_____

_____

_____

_____

_____

_____

_____

_____

_____

_____

_____

_____

_____

_____

DeAvila Bennett

The Therapeutic Journal

DeAvila Bennett

The Therapeutic Journal

_____

_____

_____

_____

_____

_____

_____

_____

_____

_____

_____

_____

_____

_____

_____

_____

_____

_____

DeAvila Bennett

The Therapeutic Journal

PROMPT #5

How was your relationship with both parents growing up?

How have the relationships impacted you?

DeAvila Bennett

The Therapeutic Journal

_____

_____

_____

_____

_____

_____

_____

_____

_____

_____

_____

_____

_____

_____

_____

_____

_____

_____

DeAvila Bennett

The Therapeutic Journal

_____

_____

_____

_____

_____

_____

_____

_____

_____

_____

_____

_____

_____

_____

_____

_____

DeAvila Bennett

The Therapeutic Journal

_____

_____

_____

_____

_____

_____

_____

_____

_____

_____

_____

_____

_____

_____

_____

_____

_____

DeAvila Bennett

PROMPT #6

What are you ready to let go
of (a terrible break-up,
failing at something, etc.)
that you feel is keeping you
from living your best life?

DeAvila Bennett

The Therapeutic Journal

DeAvila Bennett

The Therapeutic Journal

_____

_____

_____

_____

_____

_____

_____

_____

_____

_____

_____

_____

_____

_____

_____

_____

DeAvila Bennett

The Therapeutic Journal

DeAvila Bennett

The Therapeutic Journal

PROMPT #7

Think about your last painful experience (death of a loved one, break-up, something deemed as a failure).

Did you or your personality change because of that situation?

DeAvila Bennett

The Therapeutic Journal

_____

_____

_____

_____

_____

_____

_____

_____

_____

_____

_____

_____

_____

_____

_____

_____

_____

DeAvila Bennett

The Therapeutic Journal

DeAvila Bennett

The Therapeutic Journal

_____

_____

_____

_____

_____

_____

_____

_____

_____

_____

_____

_____

_____

_____

_____

_____

DeAvila Bennett

PROMPT #8

What lesson did you have to learn the hard way?

DeAvila Bennett

The Therapeutic Journal

_____

_____

_____

_____

_____

_____

_____

_____

_____

_____

_____

_____

_____

_____

_____

_____

DeAvila Bennett

The Therapeutic Journal

DeAvila Bennett

The Therapeutic Journal

_____

_____

_____

_____

_____

_____

_____

_____

_____

_____

_____

_____

_____

_____

_____

_____

_____

DeAvila Bennett

The Therapeutic Journal

PROMPT #9

What do you desire to have healing from?

DeAvila Bennett

The Therapeutic Journal

_____

_____

_____

_____

_____

_____

_____

_____

_____

_____

_____

_____

_____

_____

_____

_____

_____

DeAvila Bennett

The Therapeutic Journal

DeAvila Bennett

The Therapeutic Journal

_____

_____

_____

_____

_____

_____

_____

_____

_____

_____

_____

_____

_____

_____

_____

_____

_____

DeAvila Bennett

PROMPT #10

What makes it difficult for you to forgive yourself?

What makes it difficult for you to forgive others?

DeAvila Bennett

The Therapeutic Journal

_____

_____

_____

_____

_____

_____

_____

_____

_____

_____

_____

_____

_____

_____

_____

_____

_____

_____

DeAvila Bennett

The Therapeutic Journal

_____

_____

_____

_____

_____

_____

_____

_____

_____

_____

_____

_____

_____

_____

_____

_____

_____

DeAvila Bennett

The Therapeutic Journal

_____

_____

_____

_____

_____

_____

_____

_____

_____

_____

_____

_____

_____

_____

_____

_____

_____

DeAvila Bennett

PROMPT #11

What secrets do you keep bottled in and pray that no one ever finds out?

DeAvila Bennett

The Therapeutic Journal

_____

_____

_____

_____

_____

_____

_____

_____

_____

_____

_____

_____

_____

_____

_____

_____

DeAvila Bennett

The Therapeutic Journal

_____

_____

_____

_____

_____

_____

_____

_____

_____

_____

_____

_____

_____

_____

_____

_____

_____

DeAvila Bennett

The Therapeutic Journal

DeAvila Bennett

PROMPT #12

When other individuals
(family, friends, etc.)
state comments about
you (both positive and
negative), do you believe
what they tell you?

DeAvila Bennett

_____

_____

_____

_____

_____

_____

_____

_____

_____

_____

_____

_____

_____

_____

_____

_____

The Therapeutic Journal

_____

_____

_____

_____

_____

_____

_____

_____

_____

_____

_____

_____

_____

_____

_____

_____

_____

_____

DeAvila Bennett

The Therapeutic Journal

DeAvila Bennett

The Therapeutic Journal

DeAvila Bennett

Present

DeAvila Bennett

PROMPT #13

Who are the people who make up your support circle?

How did you choose them?

DēAvila Bennett

The Therapeutic Journal

DeAvila Bennett

The Therapeutic Journal

DeAvila Bennett

The Therapeutic Journal

DeAvila Bennett

PROMPT #14

What social messages do you feel are forced on you to conform to (going to college, getting married by a certain age, making a certain amount of money, etc.)?

Do you feel a need to conform to them? Why or why not?

DeAvila Bennett

The Therapeutic Journal

DeAvila Bennett

The Therapeutic Journal

_____

_____

_____

_____

_____

_____

_____

_____

_____

_____

_____

_____

_____

_____

_____

_____

DeAvila Bennett

The Therapeutic Journal

DeAvila Bennett

PROMPT #15

What are your beliefs about your worth?

Where/Who did you get these beliefs from?

DeAvila Bennett

The Therapeutic Journal

DeAvila Bennett

The Therapeutic Journal

DeAvila Bennett

The Therapeutic Journal

DeAvila Bennett

PROMPT #16

What are you grateful for?

DeAvila Bennett

The Therapeutic Journal

DeAvila Bennett

The Therapeutic Journal

DeAvila Bennett

The Therapeutic Journal

DeAvila Bennett

PROMPT #17

What does happiness look like to you?

DeAvila Bennett

The Therapeutic Journal

_____

_____

_____

_____

_____

_____

_____

_____

_____

_____

_____

_____

_____

_____

_____

_____

_____

_____

DeAvila Bennett

The Therapeutic Journal

DeAvila Bennett

The Therapeutic Journal

_____

_____

_____

_____

_____

_____

_____

_____

_____

_____

_____

_____

_____

_____

_____

_____

DeAvila Bennett

PROMPT #18

What do you love about yourself?

DeAvila Bennett

The Therapeutic Journal

DeAvila Bennett

The Therapeutic Journal

_____

_____

_____

_____

_____

_____

_____

_____

_____

_____

_____

_____

_____

_____

_____

_____

DeAvila Bennett

The Therapeutic Journal

_____

_____

_____

_____

_____

_____

_____

_____

_____

_____

_____

_____

_____

_____

_____

_____

_____

DeAvila Bennett

PROMPT #19

Do you understand why you handle certain situations the way you do?

Do you get angry quickly, shut-down, retaliate?

DeAvila Bennett

The Therapeutic Journal

DeAvila Bennett

The Therapeutic Journal

DeAvila Bennett

The Therapeutic Journal

_____

_____

_____

_____

_____

_____

_____

_____

_____

_____

_____

_____

_____

_____

_____

_____

_____

_____

DeAvila Bennett

PROMPT #20

Think about a time when you are free from doing anything and can process your thoughts.

What are the thoughts swimming in your head during that time?

DeAvila Bennett

The Therapeutic Journal

DeAvila Bennett

The Therapeutic Journal

DeAvila Bennett

The Therapeutic Journal

_____

_____

_____

_____

_____

_____

_____

_____

_____

_____

_____

_____

_____

_____

_____

_____

_____

DeAvila Bennett

PROMPT #21

What do your pray for?

DeAvila Bennett

The Therapeutic Journal

DeAvila Bennett

The Therapeutic Journal

DeAvila Bennett

The Therapeutic Journal

DeAvila Bennett

PROMPT #22

What are some recurrent thoughts you often have?

What feelings do you associate with those thoughts?

DeAvila Bennett

The Therapeutic Journal

DeAvila Bennett

The Therapeutic Journal

DeAvila Bennett

The Therapeutic Journal

DeAvila Bennett

PROMPT #23

What was something positive that happened to you this week?

How did it impact the rest of your week?

DeAvila Bennett

The Therapeutic Journal

_____

_____

_____

_____

_____

_____

_____

_____

_____

_____

_____

_____

_____

_____

_____

_____

_____

DeAvila Bennett

The Therapeutic Journal

_____

_____

_____

_____

_____

_____

_____

_____

_____

_____

_____

_____

_____

_____

_____

_____

_____

DeAvila Bennett

The Therapeutic Journal

_____

_____

_____

_____

_____

_____

_____

_____

_____

_____

_____

_____

_____

_____

_____

_____

_____

DeAvila Bennett

The Therapeutic Journal

PROMPT #24

What is causing you anxiety right now?

How are you coping with it?

DeAvila Bennett

The Therapeutic Journal

_____

_____

_____

_____

_____

_____

_____

_____

_____

_____

_____

_____

_____

_____

_____

_____

_____

DeAvila Bennett

The Therapeutic Journal

_____

_____

_____

_____

_____

_____

_____

_____

_____

_____

_____

_____

_____

_____

_____

_____

_____

DeAvila Bennett

The Therapeutic Journal

DeAvila Bennett

The Therapeutic Journal

Future

DeAvila Bennett

PROMPT #25

What are some goals you have set for yourself?

Where do you see yourself in 10 years?

DeAvila Bennett

The Therapeutic Journal

_____

_____

_____

_____

_____

_____

_____

_____

_____

_____

_____

_____

_____

_____

_____

_____

_____

_____

_____

DeAvila Bennett

The Therapeutic Journal

DeAvila Bennett

The Therapeutic Journal

DeAvila Bennett

PROMPT #26

What if you went to sleep and a miracle happens overnight where all your problems have been solved.

When you wake up the next morning, what would you notice that would let you know it happened?

DeAvila Bennett

The Therapeutic Journal

DeAvila Bennett

The Therapeutic Journal

DeAvila Bennett

The Therapeutic Journal

DeAvila Bennett

PROMPT #27

Why do you think you were created?

DeAvila Bennett

_____

_____

_____

_____

_____

_____

_____

_____

_____

_____

_____

_____

_____

_____

_____

_____

The Therapeutic Journal

DeAvila Bennett

The Therapeutic Journal

DeAvila Bennett

_____

_____

_____

_____

_____

_____

_____

_____

_____

_____

_____

_____

_____

_____

_____

_____

The Therapeutic Journal

_____

_____

_____

_____

_____

_____

_____

_____

_____

_____

_____

_____

_____

_____

_____

_____

DeAvila Bennett

PROMPT #28

What legacy would you like to be known for?

DeAvila Bennett

The Therapeutic Journal

_____

_____

_____

_____

_____

_____

_____

_____

_____

_____

_____

_____

_____

_____

_____

_____

_____

DeAvila Bennett

The Therapeutic Journal

_____

_____

_____

_____

_____

_____

_____

_____

_____

_____

_____

_____

_____

_____

_____

_____

_____

DeAvila Bennett

The Therapeutic Journal

DeAvila Bennett

PROMPT #29

How could you add joy into your daily life?

DeAvila Bennett

The Therapeutic Journal

DeAvila Bennett

The Therapeutic Journal

_____

_____

_____

_____

_____

_____

_____

_____

_____

_____

_____

_____

_____

_____

_____

_____

_____

DeAvila Bennett

The Therapeutic Journal

_____

_____

_____

_____

_____

_____

_____

_____

_____

_____

_____

_____

_____

_____

_____

_____

_____

_____

DeAvila Bennett

PROMPT #30

What do you need to give yourself permission to do (be more outspoken, learning to say no, forgiving yourself, etc.)?

DeAvila Bennett

The Therapeutic Journal

_____

_____

_____

_____

_____

_____

_____

_____

_____

_____

_____

_____

_____

_____

_____

_____

_____

DeAvila Bennett

The Therapeutic Journal

_____

_____

_____

_____

_____

_____

_____

_____

_____

_____

_____

_____

_____

_____

_____

_____

DeAvila Bennett

The Therapeutic Journal

_____

_____

_____

_____

_____

_____

_____

_____

_____

_____

_____

_____

_____

_____

_____

_____

_____

DeAvila Bennett

Now That You Have Finished the Journal

Well, you have made it to the end of the journal. And as great of an accomplishment that is (and it really is!), you have only just begun your journey to self-awareness and self-love.

Take this time to reflect on some or all of your completed journal entries. Ask yourself, did you discover some past hurts that you still may not have healed from? Do you have a desire to tackle them and release the hold these hurts may have on you?

I suggest if your hurts surrounded any areas of abuse, abandonment, rejection, etc., then possibly speaking with a Licensed Therapist could aid you in the next part of your journey of healing. There is nothing wrong with attending therapy and you should not feel ashamed. Most affordable therapists in your area could be found at www.psychologytoday.com.

If you are not ready to open up to someone about it or feel that your hurts are not impacting your current mental health, then just continue to grow in your identity. The "Future" section probed questions that made you think about your goals and purpose in life. You now have a mini-outline about what you may want to do. Go for it! Research. Travel. Explore. You are now taking control of your life.

May you continue to grow in your identity and love yourself flaws and all.

The Therapeutic Journal

96136661R00155

Made in the USA
Columbia, SC
21 May 2018